The Nickname
That Didn't Stick

Dedication

I dedicate this book to my wife as she has everything to do with my success. There have been many great people who have come, and gone, in my life but she has always stood by my side. No one has had more of an impact on my personal development. I am honored and blessed to be able to call her mine.

Table of Contents

1. Realizing Purpose
2. The First Nickname
3. Winning The Fight... Did I Really Win?
4. The Power of Choices
5. It Gets Worse Before It Gets Better
6. Change is Difficult
7. Failing Again and Again
8. Committed to Change
9. Meeting the Most Influential Person
10. Learning to Excel
11. Life Can Be Tough - Be Relentless

Chapter 1

Realizing Purpose

"No one cares how much you know, until they know how much you care"
- Theodore Roosevelt

I was nervous when he asked me to share my story. My first thought was, "Why would anyone want to hear from me?" All of my life I had been criticized and put down for many things I had said and now I was going to speak to a room full of people who wanted to be motivated. This seemed as though it was going to be the toughest thing I'll ever have gone through, and I have been through a lot. The only reason I accepted his request was because he was my mentor and I trusted that he knew what he was doing.

Michael was a motivational speaker and his nickname was Mr. Passion. His success had influenced the lives of many as it did mine. He wanted to meet with me due to the success I was having and ask me questions that had me talking about my childhood. The more intrigued he became, the more questions he would have. My life story moved him so much he said, "Others must hear this story. I want you to speak at the next event and share what you told me within a twenty minute time frame. Can you do that?" I answered, "Sure, I guess." He replied, "I love how relentless you were in not allowing your life to hold you back and I am certain others will feel the same!"

I wanted to believe him but I doubted that others would be interested because I lacked confidence in my speaking abilities. I was determined to satisfy his request and I wouldn't dare let him down. That night I began to write notes for the next event, which was a week away, and tried to figure out how to squeeze it into a twenty-minute message. When I felt it was complete, I was still uneasy about how others may think less of me. It was all I had so I stuck it in my briefcase. I was determined to use my fear as energy and deliver the message anyway.

When I arrived at the next event, I was surprised at the turnout as there was a big crowd. When everyone looked up at me I thought, "I can't do this. They'll laugh at me. They'll think I am a big dummy." These thoughts almost made me leave the room but I ignored these feelings and made myself sit down. When Michael got to the stage and looked over at me, I almost passed out. He started talking about me in such a positive way that my spirits were lifted and I felt the energy to start making my way up. Then he introduced me by saying, "Please - welcome to the stage, Mr. Relentless, Jim Beach!"

The applause fired me up and I gained a little more confidence. I ran with the energy and barely used my notes. I can't even remember if I stayed within my time but it didn't seem that Michael was bothered by it. I poured my heart out and expressed that I have been at the point of giving up so many times in my life but I just couldn't. There was a burning desire to be better than what I was told I would ever be. Some of the struggles I have had would've been considered good enough excuses to give up and quit in the eyes of others.

I have experienced the success that others told me I would never have because of my relentless effort to apply the personal development I have learned over the years. I finally told the people that attended the event, that the results I had created were not because I have talent. I told them that anyone can have the same, as long as they were relentless about what is possible. When I placed the microphone down and motioned for Michael to take over, people began to applaud and even thanked me for sharing. I couldn't believe the results.

At the close of the event, there were several people who came straight over to speak with me. One man in particular, with tears in his eyes, came to me and said, "Young man, what you shared today has completely changed my life and I want to thank you!" This is where I realized my purpose and accepted the new nickname I was given. I then embarked on a journey that has led me to write this book.

I have looked back and asked myself if I would change anything and I would answer, "No" as the past helped me to discover a relentless passion to help others. There are so many who are stuck living by the nicknames they have been given. They have no idea that it's possible to become more, and be great, as greatness lives in each of us.

Chapter 2

The First Nickname

"Think twice before you speak, because your words and influence will plant the seed of either success or failure in the mind of another." - Napoleon Hill

Growing up in Las Vegas, Nevada was quite an experience, especially while having deaf parents. A busy place with a lot of people and my parents did just fine in a hearing world. I didn't do so well. I could hear but my first language was American Sign Language. I could speak some words but I couldn't speak in complete sentences. This caused a lot of confusion with everyone I would meet and I was often misunderstood.

Starting school was a nightmare. The kids would pick on me and in many situations, I was bullied. I wanted to fit in but I couldn't communicate that to the other kids. Before long, they started calling me "Retard". The nickname didn't take long to spread through the school. There were many games, requiring strategy, where all the kids would get picked and I would be left standing by myself. If I was the last pick they would say, "I don't want the Retard!" I was fairly athletic but was always slow to pick up the rules to the activity in which I was involved. I'd get so mad and I was often disciplined for fighting and sent to the Principal's office. After just a couple visits, he asked my parents to meet with him.

The fact that I couldn't communicate other than with my hands, facial expressions and body language caused the school officials concern. They told my parents that there were no special programs that would fit my particular needs and that I may have a severe learning disability or that I was possibly mentally handicapped. The hour long meeting ended with the Principal suggesting that I just do the best I can and they would pass me from one grade to the next anyway.

I left that day believing them because I considered them the experts and trusted that they knew what they were talking about. This didn't make things any easier. Rather, it caused me to become bitter and often ask, "Why do I have to be different?" I still wanted to fit in and be what others called normal so I did what I could with my social life. I tried so hard that I was often picked on for being an attention seeker.

As I got older, I could speak a little better but never well enough to rid me of my awful nickname. I was bullied often and to the point that I asked my parents to enroll me in a karate school. They denied my request and explained that they couldn't afford it. I tried teaching myself by watching all the great karate movies that came out in the 70's and 80's but it didn't help much. Finally, I called a school and explained my financial situation and offered to do janitorial work in trade for lessons. They accepted and even gave me my first karate uniform for free.

The physical bullying wasn't as much of a problem after I started training. However, I was still picked on and the name calling didn't cease. I wasn't going to fight and get kicked out of school so I just let them talk. The words I would hear would eat away at me little by little but there was little I could do. If I told a teacher, I got picked on for being a tattle tale and threatened if I were to ever do it again.

This wasn't something I only experienced at school as I was just as picked on by other kids at my local church. The church was a better place as far as the adults were concerned but I still couldn't fit in with kids my own age. They would call me Retard as well. I would play with the younger kids as they were more accepting. I was often asked why I talked so strange and I would always say, "I don't talk strange. You do." That usually got a laugh and we would just move on.

The adults were often rude or would ignore me due to my strange communication skills. This only made me more bitter and I would act out so that I could get their attention. Even though I would get some kind of discipline, I would accept it as interaction. Many would say that I was hyper and would put me in time out. When that didn't work they'd send me to my parents. I felt bad as it stressed my parents but I was still trying to figure things out.

Some adults, because of my immaturity, feel that they could take advantage of me and would in some cases. One particular man, who had a sexual interest in young boys, tried his best to prey upon me. I had no idea that he was preparing an attempt to take advantage. He would give me money, many were special coins, in order to make me like and spend time with him - it worked. Conversations were limited for the obvious reasons but was also what saved me. I decided to go to an adult I trusted and told them who he was, what he was saying and that he was giving me money. That person asked me to stay away from him. I didn't understand why but I obeyed. Evidently, someone went and talked with him asking him to leave and never come back because, after that day, I don't remember ever seeing him again.

Trying to comprehend what happened during that time was not important to me. I was still of the belief that I was of a lesser intelligence and it wasn't for me to understand. This is how I would treat everything in life, including my school work. There were a few teachers who would try to reach out to me but I would reject them. At that time, no one would be able to convince me that I could do any better academically and I wouldn't listen if they tried. There were some, well meaning, kids who tried to help and I would engage but only in an attempt to make a friend. Because of this, I suffered in my early years of education.

What I hope that others can learn from this part of my life is that we will become what we believe of ourselves. Others will always have opinions but we never have to accept their beliefs! Happiness, joy, energy and a vigor for life is going to be up to you. How you choose to incorporate these characteristics are imperative to living a productive and positive life. You do not have to make the same mistakes I did, however, you can learn from them so as to not repeat these experiences. I didn't learn this until later in life and will share how I came to discover the truth.

Chapter 3

Winning The Fight… Did I Really Win?

***"You may have to fight a battle more than once to win it."* - Margaret Thatcher**

    I was finally getting fed up with how others viewed me and decided to make changes that would change everything. My efforts seemed to be working as I started to improve in school by doing the best I could to complete assignments and actually doing my homework. Little by little, I felt I was actually improving my intelligence even though I didn't have anyone saying they noticed. This was frustrating but I kept trying. I would involve myself in church functions and become more involved in the youth activities. Things were starting to pick up and I was feeling a little better about myself.

    The bullying was dwindling slowly but I was still trying to figure out how to eliminate it altogether. The adults in the church and my teachers were complimenting me on my improved behaviors but I couldn't seem to make things change with my peers. At that time, I would have rather had the other kids noticing and accepting this change than anyone else. However, it didn't seem to be working. I guess they just looked at how I used to be and believed I would never change. This would depress me and cause me to become bitter again. I decided to just be the quiet kid and this led to my being an introvert. The more I kept to myself, the less I was getting picked on. So, I continued to keep to myself. This didn't help my belief that I was still a retard and that I would ever become anything more.

The more I kept to myself, I was able to focus more on my academics and even started to pull up a grade or two. I was able to do this for a short while until my inferiority complex got the best of me. The kids in school would still find ways to pick on me regardless of how quiet I became. Then one day, I just had enough of the bullying when one of the toughest gangbangers in our school chose to embarrass me in front of the whole class. I was trying to obey my father's request to never fight in school but this guy really made me angry. I was sharpening a pencil when he decided to pick on me. He pushed me into the pencil sharpener, which I hit with my face, causing other students to laugh at me.

When I turned around, I shoved him and he fell over the teacher's desk. The teacher stood up but she wasn't the only one. There were other gangbangers, of which were his friends, that stood up as though they were going to come to his defense. I yelled out, "Wait! I don't want to fight you at school. You know where I live so just come to my house and I will fight you there!" I didn't think before I spoke but I was already committed. I wasn't going to back down, not this time, as I was ready to end the bullying. I thought to myself, "Even if I lose this fight, I will still earn the respect of others and they will know not to mess with me anymore!" Boy, was I wrong!

When I got home, I told my dad what happened. I said, "You asked me not to fight in school and I almost did. I stopped by asking him to fight me here at home and he agreed." My dad thought I was just kidding and said, "Then I'll help you get prepared. Let's go outside and I'll show you a thing or two." My dad was a little guy and never had the martial arts training that I did. However, he was all the support I had at the moment and I wasn't going to turn him down. We went out to the front yard and began sparring. All of the sudden, my dad's face changed when he looked over my shoulder. I turned to see what he was looking at and noticed that the gangbanger accepted my request and was headed to my house. He wasn't alone.

Walking with him was what seemed to be fifty or more other kids, as well as several grown-ups, walking down the street. They were all shouting and supporting him. I felt all alone and for the first time, I was scared for my life. I started to walk inside when a couple of guys shouted out to me and said, "Hey, don't worry. We are here to support you and we are not going to allow anyone else to jump in. This is a one on one fight and we're going to make sure it stays that way." With that, I felt a little more confident that everything was going to be okay so I walked out to the yard and said, "Okay, let's fight!"

Neither of us wanted to throw the first punch

so we just stood there shouting at each other for a while until the crowd started screaming, "Fight!" A girl, tomboy, came up from behind and tried to get the fight started by pushing me into my opponent. It didn't work and my mom, sweetest person you'll ever hope to meet, chased her out of the yard. Others yelled at that girl and told her to stay out of it. When I turned to look at the gangbanger, he was headed towards me and tackled me as though we were playing football. His arms got stuck under me and I began to start punching.

      I don't remember much of this part of the fight, other than throwing flying kicks and feeling rage unlike ever before. Last thing I remember was having others trying to tear us apart and shouting, "Stop! You're killing him!" That's when I noticed I had my hands around his throat and was choking him. I wasn't looking to kill anybody so I let go. As he walked away, other fights began to happen in the crowd of people as though we encouraged others to fight. People were shouting praises to me as the winner of the fight and doing the opposite to the gangbanger. This made me feel like a champion and I believed that it has helped me to gain the respect I deserved. It wasn't until the next day that I realized I was wrong.

      As I walked down the school halls, there were people I didn't even know calling out to me and saying things like, "Good job" and "Way to go!" I felt as though I was finally getting out of being bullied and was going to make new friends. However, throughout the day, I kept hearing the rumors that the gangbanger and his gang were planning on coming after me. Confused, I asked myself, "Why? If I won then shouldn't that have settled it?" I couldn't answer that question so I asked others and many responded with, "I think you better get in a gang of your own so that you have protection." So, that's just what I did and it was the worst mistake of my life!

Sometimes we listen to others, especially when we feel that our time is limited, but we don't look for the right people in which to listen. We could always look back and say what happened was their fault but then we don't take responsibility for our own actions and we won't make the right changes. We all have the right resources and people in our lives but we are not patient enough to do the research. That leads to more problems. The sooner we realize it, the better life will become and the less problems we have. I wished I would have learned this earlier but I didn't and life became more difficult. Learn from my experience and make the right choices.

Chapter 4

The Power of Choices

"There are three constants in life... change, choice and principles." - Stephen Covey

My search for a gang to be a part of didn't take long because I was living in Las Vegas and gangs were everywhere. I didn't know what to expect and all I wanted was the protection but that's not the reality. When you join a gang, there are things that will be required of you. Failure to accept the rules will get you a beating, and in some cases, death. These were things I learned after joining.

The day that I joined, we had a meeting and I met some guys no one would ever want in their lives. They gathered around me and started shouting, "Do you really want to be in a gang?" I replied. "Yes!" Then they started beating on me. I fought back the best I could but there was more than I could handle. As quickly as it started, it was over. Next was all the hugs and the congratulations for being a part of "The Family". They would begin to tell me that no one else will love me more than my brothers and that I was a part of the family for life.

I was so excited that when I got home, I told my dad. That wasn't the best idea but how was I to know? He said, "Son, I am not okay with that and as long as you're in a gang I want nothing to do with you!" He was trying to show me tough love but I didn't understand how tough love worked and I resented him for it. From that day on, my dad and I did not get along. We fought and argued all of the time and often avoided each other. He tried to get people from our church to talk with me but it didn't do any good and I then decided that I wouldn't go back to the church. At first, my dad would force me to go but some would tell him that if he forced me I would resent the church and never go back. So, he left me alone.

My mom had a different strategy and it would work, sometimes. She would simply ask me to join them and if I said no, she would just smile and say, "Okay, maybe next time". She was the sweetest person I knew so I didn't want to disappoint her all the time. My gang life bothered her but she wouldn't fight me over it and tried her best to be patient with me. This was hard for her because she had to witness a lot of things that no one would ever want to see. There were many times that I would come home bloody and bruised and she would tend to my wounds.

Joining the gang so that I would have protection from the gangbanger that I first fought was my ultimate goal but little did I know I would get into a lot more fights and need even more protection. Wasn't long before my little brother decided that he wanted to join a gang as well. I didn't try to stop him and that's when things got even worse. We were introduced to sex, drugs and alcohol. These things seemed cool and we didn't think much about it being wrong. We were meeting all kinds of new people. We thought were a part of the cool crowd and that was something we never knew.

Being involved in all of these activities led me back to failing in school and neglecting to do right in my life. I didn't quit going but I just sat in class and did nothing as I was allowed to do in the past. Few teachers noticed the change and tried to reach out but I was just not going to listen. I was finally getting the attention and respect I thought I deserved by being in a gang. It was a place I thought I fit in because I didn't have to be intelligent and I didn't have to speak well. I didn't require an education to be involved and I was capable of following through when the gang needed me. The feeling of being needed was enough for me to stick around.

Being a "thug" also seemed like a cool thing and I cannot deny that sometimes we had fun. I would have new experiences and make new, so called, friends of which some of them became lifelong friends because they made changes in their lives as well. The music we listened to as gangbangers was entertaining. However, it did encourage a lot of bad behaviors and helped us to come up with ideas to do more wrong.

Since I was bullied so much of my childhood, I

decided to bully others because then I would feel as though I would no longer be a victim. I didn't think that I was making a victim of others, at that time, because it was my defense. I couldn't see past my pain to notice the pain of others. I was fighting often and, because of my martial arts training, I was winning most of the fights. I was becoming fearless, regardless of their size and strength, and that eventually cause me to get hurt in ways that I would never wish on anyone.

After some time, I learned that the love of your gang members was mixed with a lot of pain. If we were perceived to have disrespected the leader, or a fellow member, in any way - we would get a beating from a multitude of members at a time. Due to this, I now have a permanent discoloration of the skin around my eye. I live with that as a reminder of their, so called, love.

I have had so many close encounters with death. I have had days of overdose, guns to the head and have been shot at a number of times. I've had knives pulled on me as well as many other weapons. A memory I will never forget is having a gun with a laser beam pointed in my eye from 10 feet away. This person would constantly switch from eye to eye to let me know that if he pulled the trigger, he wouldn't miss.

I've had friends who have been shot and killed, one by the police. Some who've died by overdose and some who have ended up with a permanent residence in a mental hospital. Some who are homeless and cannot be found. Friends who were victims of rape and one in particular was raped, killed and thrown in an open Las Vegas desert. She was found by a kid and his grandfather as reported by the local news.

I could go on and on about all of the things that happened by way of the gang but that would be a complete book in itself. The point I am making, by sharing what I have, is to show that most all of the choices we make will lead us down a path we have made for ourselves and we must live with that and take personal responsibility.

I had tried to get involved in other activities that were more respectable. Once, I become a part of a juggling crew and juggled at the Excalibur Casino. I was an assistant to a magician and helped with magic shows for several casinos. I became a part of a Hip Hop dance crew, and this group was intent on being clean from all illegal drugs. These things did keep me away from the gang but I would eventually fall back into trouble and neglect the duties of all the other activities because I never felt I deserved the good that was coming in my life.

The lessons I learned from all of these things didn't hit me until I made a radical change but what I came to understand is I am the one who made the choices. If I would have stuck with the more positive choices, things might have turned around much earlier and I wouldn't have suffered so much.

Choices, whether major or minor, must be evaluated so as to make the right decision when an important choice is to be made.

Chapter 5

It Gets Worse Before It Gets Better

"Our greatest weakness lies in giving up. The most certain way to succeed is always to try just one more time." - Thomas A. Edison

The fights, the drugs and the yard parties got to be too much for my dad to handle. I didn't think much of it until I came home to celebrate my 18th birthday with my family and found a moving truck sitting in the driveway. I was confused because I didn't know my parents were planning to move. I ran straight to my mom and asked her what was going on. With tears in her eyes, she said, "You'll have to go ask your dad." I looked until I found him in the back of the moving truck. He was sweating profusely as he was trying to move things as fast as possible. He wanted to get done as quickly as possible so I didn't try to talk him out of it and it worked.

I got his attention and asked, "Why are you moving?" His reply was, "Son, I have asked you to change your ways and you wouldn't listen. I don't want to live in Las Vegas anymore because of all the trouble you are causing here. I want to move to Kansas and find other deaf people to mingle with and have a fresh start. You are 18 years old today and I am going to give you a choice. I am offering to let you move with us but you will have to get out of the gang and stop doing drugs. It's time you cleaned up your life. Now, if you choose not to accept then you can stay here in Las Vegas. I will give you a check so that you can pay your first month's rent as well as your first month's worth of groceries but after that, you are on your own. What will it be?"

I was enraged because this was all happening so fast and all that I could think about was that I would be leaving behind my friends and the only life I knew. So I just said, "I'll take that check because I am not going anywhere!" I snatched the check from his hand and went inside to complain to my mother and brother. They were not looking forward to it as much as my dad was and my brother was actually angry.

When we all said our goodbyes, I stood in the street and watched as they took off for their new life. What hurt the worst at that moment was to see my youngest brother cry as he stared at me from the back window of mom's car. As soon as I lost sight of them, I turned around and looked at my old neighborhood and realized that I wouldn't be living here anymore either. I wanted to be excited that I was now on my own but I was also scared because I didn't know where to go.

    I headed over to a friend's house to share my circumstance and on the way, I thought long and hard about where I was going to live. Would I live by myself or should I move in with somebody and pay rent? Would anyone want me to live with them? How long will it take to find someone to help me and would they be willing? The more I thought, the more scared I got. Yeah, you could say I was a tough guy because I was a gangbanger but then again, I was still only a teen - and now without any parental guidance. Then again, even adults find themselves afraid when they are in a place of uncertainty.

The friend I was going to see wasn't home and had no plans of returning anytime soon. Now I was really beginning to freak out. I walked a mile to a gas station to use a payphone and began calling all the friends I thought might care and be willing to help. I had to call collect because all I had was a check. Many refused the collect calls and now I was not only scared but I started to become angry. Finally, I made contact with a friend who was willing to help out and they came to pick me up.

After I shared all my troubles, the friend accepted to let me live with them and pay rent. The only requirement was that I needed to get a job to help pay the living expenses. I agreed and was hopeful for what I thought would be a new start in my life. For the first month, we had a great time partying on the money my dad had given to me. When the money was running out, I began to search for a job. I dressed the best I could but as a gangbanger my clothing choices were limited and not very appealing to any employer. No one called me and offered me a job.

At this point, I decided to work for myself and begin selling drugs. This only helped for a short time as I had a problem with using the drugs I was supposed to be selling. Then I became an addict with a serious drug use problem. I was getting so bad that the person I was living with said that if I didn't change my ways, she would kick me out. I got mad as though she was no longer the understanding friend she presented herself to be. I couldn't see that the problem was me so I argued my situation and only made it worse. She gave me a time frame in which to change and get a real job. I couldn't meet the demands and it was finally time to go.

I left with a small backpack that only had a few things and my small childhood dog. By this time, I had been hooked on meth for about seven to eight months and was a serious addict. I took the bus and walked as much as I could until I got to my old neighborhood. I looked to talk to some old friends but some of them left for college and others just moved out on their own. The friends I did find just gave me a little money, asked me to spend it on food and asked that I never come back because they didn't like what I had become. This is when I finally realized I was a homeless person.

I had too much pride to call dad and let him know that he was right about all my friends and to ask him to let me come home so I just decided to live on the streets. My thought was that surely if I was to make it being homeless, I was living in the best city in which to do so. Again, I took the bus and walked until I got to the Las Vegas Strip. This is where I was going to do my begging for money and food since this is where all the tourists with money would be.

    I was embarrassed at first but that faded quickly because the tourists didn't know me. The money I would get wasn't much but I was able to buy enough food to feed my dog. I would feed her first because I didn't want to see her die before me if we were not going to survive. We would sleep on casino lawns until we were kicked off the property. The hardest moment I had with being homeless was how dirty and nasty I looked to the public. I remember a time where a woman and her daughter, walking on the same sidewalk, crossed the street only to cross back over when she got passed me.
    I was now totally disgusted with myself as I couldn't get a shower, sleep in a comfortable bed or enjoy some real company. I decided it was time to try living again and reach out to someone who could help me to clean up my life completely and if I couldn't - I was going to just give up. I believed there was more for me but this time I needed to find the people that would believe the same. I didn't want any more handouts and I truly wanted change so I started to look for a church.

Chapter 6

Change is Difficult

"You must take personal responsibility. You cannot change the circumstances, the seasons, or the wind, but you can change yourself. That is something you have charge of." - Jim Rohn

Walking was all I could afford but I was willing to take the journey to a church I was familiar with and I believed could help. Eighteen miles later, I finally arrived. No one was around but the sign said there would be a church service that evening so I waited. As I sat there, I visited with my dog and thought about what I would say to the pastor. I figured if the church can't help me, there would be someone there that could. My thoughts were interrupted by the sound of the first car that pulled into the church parking lot.

It was someone I didn't know and I tried to stay out of sight. I didn't want to be seen until I recognized someone and believed they would be a little understanding. I ended up waiting until church had started before I snuck in. A few stares and a few smiles were given as I made my way to the back pew. I don't remember if I listened to the preacher as I was more focused on how I would explain myself. I was uncomfortable because of the way I looked and the shame I carried. However, I wasn't going to leave until I found the help.

Finally, the pastor closed the service and dismissed the people. I made my way to the people I picked out and became discouraged with each encounter as they would each give me a reason as to why they couldn't help me. I didn't blame them as they each had legitimate reasons. After I reached the last person I could think of, I decided to leave. I have never been suicidal but as I began to make my way out to the end of the parking lot, I began to consider suicide. Then I heard someone call out my name. When I turned around, I saw Mike. He was someone I knew but didn't think would help because he didn't know me well enough.

"I heard you were asking for help and wanted to make a change. Did you mean that?' asked Mike. I answered, "Yes! I really do want to change. I am tired of living the way that I do." He replied, "Come with me. I'll get you some food and you can stay at my house for the night. I will take you to someone I know will help you. You must know that there will be rules. You will need to stay away from drugs and he will help you get a job." I thanked him and hopped into his truck. True to his word, he took me to a burger joint and fed me very well. I don't know if I have ever had, or will ever have, a cheeseburger that tasted that good.

When we got to his home, I stood by as he

explained to his wife why he had brought me there. She, with a smile on her face, agreed to allow me to stay. Their beautiful little girls were smiling as they told me good night. Then, he offered me a hot shower and a place to lay my head. As I laid down, all I could think about was how nice it was and how long it had been since I felt like someone cared. I felt at peace which also helped me to sleep very well that night!

The next morning, he took me to the home of a man named Russell that looked, sounded and acted just like the actor Morgan Freeman. He was classy and extremely nice. After hearing about my situation, he said he would be willing to let me stay but he had rules that I must follow. First rule was that we must read the bible and have bible discussions. All the other rules revolved around responsibilities such as getting a job and helping with the living expenses. I had no problem accepting these rules since I was looking to better my life.

Russell went to work the next day and talked with his boss about me. I stayed behind reading the "Help Wanted" ads to find work for myself in case Russell couldn't get me any work. I didn't find anything I believed I could do and everywhere I called wanted me to have a High School Diploma, which I never achieved. I was getting frustrated but I wasn't going to give up. I kept looking and making calls until Russell got home. He walked in with a smile on his face and said, "You got the job!" I was thrilled until he told me we would wake up every morning at 6:00 am. I groaned but was too happy to have a job to complain.

The next morning, we headed off to work and talked about the job we had that day. I was going to be a painter. I thought it would be pretty easy until halfway through the day. There were so many details I didn't know and the other guys would pick on me about them all. I then started getting an attitude with each of them and almost got into a few fights. Russell would pull me to the side, often, and try to help me understand what it meant to not take things so personally. This was a hard lesson to learn.

Before long, I wanted to look for another line of work and Russell said it was fine but I had to keep my job until then. I made more calls and finally one agreed to an interview. All went well and I got the job, at a local mall, as a stocker for a newly opened salsa store. I will never forget the experience as some of the things I learned still affect me in a positive way today! I enjoyed the job so much and the managers like me so well they promoted me to sales. I started to make pretty good money and began learning how to save.

One evening, I came home and found out that Russell hadn't worked that day. I asked him what happened and he told me that he, and many of the others, were laid off because work had slowed down. He assured me that it wouldn't be long before they got more work but until then he wouldn't have any money to help with the bills. So, for a month, I took care of all of the bills. This was a valuable lesson for me as I learned more about responsibilities than I had ever learned before.

Over time, I began to miss my family so I decided I would try to move to Kansas and start over there. I called my mom using a device for the deaf and told her my plans. She was excited and said she would explain everything to dad. I thanked Russell for all the things he taught me and for all the help he had given. I then made my way out the door. I rode with a friend who was already headed to Kansas and was willing to bring me along.

Chapter 7

Failing Again and Again

***"I've failed over and over and over again in my life and that is why I succeed."* - Michael Jordan**

The trip didn't go as I expected as he was headed to his family's house first. That wasn't a big deal but on the way he offered me some meth and I couldn't restrain myself. I tried but my thought was that a little couldn't hurt. This was a big mistake but I wouldn't realize it until much later. One serving wasn't enough so we just kept using and one day turned into two. I wanted to hurry and get home so I could get away from the drugs and start over again but I had no idea what was waiting for me when I got home.

Finally, I arrived. Everyone was pleased to see me and we had a great time visiting. At the end of the night, my dad wanted to talk with me. He asked me if I really did change and suggested I get a job right away. I didn't tell him about the trip home but I told him about all of the changes I did make. He was pleased and headed off to bed. My brother was outside with some friends so I went out to visit with them. Everything seemed okay at first but it wasn't long until I learned what his new friends were like.

All of his friends were cool but they were also

thugs. None of his friends were bad people but the choices they were making weren't good. After we learned enough about each other, they felt comfortable enough to pull out some marijuana and offered to share with me. Without any hesitation, I accepted, because I had been awake and wired for days. Before long, I was ready for bed and headed into my new home and went straight to my room. I layed there for a while and just before I fell asleep, I thought about what I had done and asked myself, "Did I really change or did I just fail?"

    The next day, I looked for the guys I hung out with the night before. I wanted to go have more fun and maybe even find some single girls. When we got together, I had learned that they partied every day and they were glad to have me tag along. This is where my life began to spiral out of control again but I didn't see it at the time. All I could see was that they seemed happy and I wanted share in that happiness. I had no idea that they also had troubles but I found out in a short period of time.

    The drugs and violence in Kansas City were much worse than what I had experienced in Las Vegas and once again, I felt I couldn't get away. I wasn't doing as many drugs as I had before but I found myself in more danger. I was shot at and threatened more this time so I felt that I needed protection again. The guys I hung out with had started a gang of guys who were all from a different gang background and called themselves, "The KLIK". This was to say that though we were all from different gangs, we still clicked together. I decided to join the gang and moved into one of the homes that housed many of the members. This time, my dad wasn't mad but he was disappointed. I think that hurt worse as I would have rather had him angry instead.

Shortly after I got in the gang, the main leader and several other members ended up in prison. They were caught because the KLIK made the local news. I was asked to lead the gang while the leader was away but it didn't last long because the gang started falling apart and going their separate ways. With what we had left, we just partied and continued using and selling drugs. I thought things were much safer now and we would just have fun. I was wrong.

A couple of us decided to take a trip to Oklahoma and party there for a little while. On the way there, we decided to smoke some marijuana and listen to some music. I was driving while the others fell asleep. I was listening to the music and became sleepy myself. I fell asleep at the wheel and steered off the road. I hit a guardrail going 70 miles an hour, in cruise control, and launched off into a ditch. The 1985 Honda Accord was in flames and destroyed. I was awoken and noticed that the passenger to my right was still asleep. I tried to open my door but it was jarred shut. I climbed out of the window and called to the other passenger as he started coming around.

He looked over at me and asked, "What

happened?" I said, "Don't worry about that right now. Just get out of the car!" He climbed over the seat and I pulled him out of the same window. Bloody and beaten, we headed up to the highway which was at the top of the hill. I sat down and started to pass out. I called out to my friends and asked them to keep me awake. They said they couldn't help me because they needed to figure out how to get the drugs out of the car and hide them somewhere. This is when I realized that the so called love from my gang friends wasn't that strong.

Many times, I had been close to death by murder but this was the first time I was actually afraid that I was going to die. As I started passing out, I began to pray. I asked God if he would give me another chance and I promised I would change. I feel that he granted that request because I started hearing the voices of the firemen who showed up to the scene. They asked a lot of questions but I could only remember one and that was, "Do you feel that you need to go to the hospital?" I told them I didn't even though I should have but I didn't want to look weak to the other guys. Today, as a result, I still have physical problems caused by the wreck. The next day, we were getting a lot of attention for surviving the accident but all I could think about was getting home.

When we returned to Kansas, we planned a party so we could all get high and have some fun. I remembered my promise to God but I went anyway. While at the party, I just couldn't enjoy the party as I thought I would. The promise kept popping up in my head even until after I left the party. I decided that night I would go to my parents' home to spend the night and gather my thoughts. When I got there, it was around 2:00 am. I entered and heard a voice but I wasn't sure where it was coming from. I walked through the house until I could find where and who it was. It was the voice of my mother praying.

Even though deaf people cannot speak well, if at all, I could still understand what my mother was saying. She was asking God to save my brother and me. I was heartbroken and began to pray myself and let God know that I was going to keep my promise. I went to bed thinking about how many times I have failed but still had hoped for change. I told myself that this time it wasn't going to be a small change and that it was going to be a lasting one. No more was I going to allow my failures to be excuses to make them over and over again. The next day, I was on the hunt for another church but couldn't decide where to go. I didn't and wouldn't give up until I had made that find. You only fail when you truly give up!

Chapter 8

Committed to Change

***"I believe life is constantly testing us for our level of commitment, and life's greatest rewards are reserved for those who demonstrate a never-ending commitment to act until they achieve."* - Tony Robbins**

I was riding around with a friend of the gang and we passed by a small church on a hillside and I said, "Turn around man, I just saw a church." He laughed and said, "You? Church? Yeah right!" I replied, "I'm serious! I gotta make a change bro!" He looked at me funny and said, "Okay man but only if you're serious." I gave him a serious look and he turned the truck around. As we pulled in, I was reading the sign and looking for the schedule. I found that there was a service that Wednesday night and I decided to go.

"Are you really going?" asked my friend. "Absolutely!" I replied. He then said, "You know what? I think I will go with you." We got dressed in what we considered our best and headed to the church. The people looked at us funny but treated us like family. I sat in the back and listened and the pastor said, "The title of tonight's sermon is, "Devil, you missed!" The sermon fit well to all the times the devil tried to take my life and I was moved. I wanted to go to the altar but I was too ashamed. Finally, we left but on the way out, many invited us to come back. I told them that I would and I meant it.

When I got home, I told my parents of my experience and my dad doubted that I really went to a church. I then invited him to go with me. He asked, "When is the next service?" I answered, "This Sunday. Want to come?" He agreed and promised he would go. I am sure that the only reason was to see if I was telling the truth but when Sunday rolled around I asked him if he was still going to go with me. He had a surprised but happy look on his face and said, "Yes. Let me get dressed."

This time, I sat through the sermon and didn't listen to anything. It wasn't that I did not want to receive the message but I was focused on the altar and waiting for the opportunity to go. Finally, the service came to an end but I don't remember a call to the altar. I was disappointed and started to walk out. On the way to the back door, I believe I heard the voice of God say, "If you leave now, you'll never come back." I turned, looked at the altar and asked, "Never?" Not waiting for an answer, I ran to the altar and began to weep. I was begging God for forgiveness and prayed for a very long time.

Many of the church members were praying with me. A while later, the pastor asked, "Hey… Did you mean it when you asked God to forgive you?" I answered, "Yes!" He then replied, "Then he has already forgiven you and you don't need to beg anymore. It's a beautiful thing called mercy." After hearing that, I felt joy like I had never felt before and then I was filled with the Holy Ghost as mentioned in the book of Acts from the Holy Bible. I danced and shouted with joy and the church celebrated with me.

After I was done giving praise to the Lord, I started wiping the tears from my eyes. When I was able to see again, I turned to look at who was beside me and saw that it was my dad and he was still crying. He reached out to hug me and we held each other for the first time in 7 years. We cried together for a good while and then he pulled back so that he could sign to me and said, "I am proud of you and I am excited about what the future holds!" I replied, "Yeah, me too!"

I slept well that night after thinking about all that happened that night. I woke up the next morning thinking about it all over again and was smiling from ear to ear. My parents greeted me and asked what my plans were for the day. I replied, "I am going to look for a job!" They responded, "That's a great idea!" I didn't want to just get any job but I was willing to work just about anything until I found something I could really enjoy. I decided I would pray about it and I felt at peace as though everything was going to work out for me.

Wasn't long before the church I was attending

had a revival and I had met a great guy named Dan. He owned a windows and siding company and told me he was looking for help and felt to offer me the job. I was excited and started immediately. Dan was one of the nicest guys I had ever met and was a really good boss. Every morning, he would drive over an hour just to pick me up and take me home. He liked to start each day off with prayer and that helped me with my prayer life.

During that time, God had confirmed that he had put the calling to preach on my life. The very first time I preached, I was nervous but God had given me the words to say and that sermon went very well. Before long, I was preaching out and becoming very comfortable speaking in front of others but it still didn't help with my interaction with people. I really wanted to improve my social skills and I knew it needed work. I knew that in time, by the help of God, I wouldn't be such an introvert and I would finally get over the fear.

After just a short time of working with Dan, he offered to give me a car so that I could drive myself. I was shocked but excited. I accepted and learned a great lesson on what "being a giver" really means. He saw a genuine need and had the ability to help. I truly believe it is why his business and his life was blessed. Dan later found the love of his life and had gotten married. A short time after he was married, he became a pastor. With him, I learned more than just the tricks of the trade. I was encouraged to better myself with each day I was around him and wanted to one day bless someone else like he did for me.

Things were going well for me at this time as it seemed to wake me up and create a desire to not just be alive but to really live. I wanted to do more and become more but I just didn't know how. This hunger would grow each and every day and I kept thinking of different ways to improve myself. I heard the phrase, "Good things come to those who wait", but I was not a patient person. I wanted to live a fuller life and I wanted it right now so I became relentless in doing what it takes.

Chapter 9

Meeting the Most Influential Person

"Someone's opinion of you does not have to become your reality" - Les Brown

One night at church, I went to the altar to pray and ask God to send me a girlfriend as I was ready to start dating. I looked over to the other side of the altar and I saw a beautiful woman praying with her son. Then, I believe I heard the voice of God and he said, "That is who you will marry". I argued with God because when I saw her son I said, "There's no way God… She's married!" I didn't hear anything after that but I was going to trust that I would soon find someone to date.

About a week later, that young lady came over to the other side of the church to greet me. She said, "Hi, my name is April". I then told her who I was. We chatted for just a minute or two and then she asked me if I would like to go out to dinner with her and a friend. I was shocked and speechless. She saw that I was stuck and said, "I am just asking to go out as friends". I then snapped out of it because I realized I was looking like a deer caught in the headlights and said, "Oh, uh, yeah. Of course". I tried to act a little more confident but her smile told me that I couldn't fool her.

That night, we went to an internationally known pancake house and while we were visiting she became really uncomfortable. Maybe I wasn't engaged enough in the conversation but I was struggling with the thought of sounding stupid. "What if she finds out I am not a very smart man?" I asked myself. I kept watching and noticed that she would look at me, then passed me and wondered if she was becoming disinterested and was looking for the door.

I couldn't take it anymore and decided to ask, "What's the matter?" She then told me about the guy sitting behind me and said he had been staring at her all night. "He is a scary looking man and he's making me nervous." she said. I then started to get upset and asked her if she wanted me to take care of it. She said, "No but just don't let me walk out to the car by myself." I boldly replied, "You have nothing to worry about. I will take care of you!" This helped ease her nerves, we had no problems and we continued to have a great time. That night, I believed I conveyed that I could be a great protector.

One date led to the next and I then got to meet her son, Austin. He and I connected so well that he would call me his good friend. Things just got better and better each time we got together so we started talking about taking our relationship to the next step. I told her about what I believed God had told me and she was surprised and said, "Well, I have been praying that God would send me a good husband." I smiled and said, "Oh, I..." She looked at me with a puzzled look and asked, "What's the matter?" I looked down at the ground and said, "I don't know if I could be a good husband. I was told that I have a severe learning disability and I wouldn't amount to much of anything. I didn't even graduate high school. I won't be able to get a good career and I don't know if I will ever make enough money to provide for a family."

Her response shocked me as she said, "First of all, they lied to you and secondly, what they say about you doesn't have to be your reality. I believe in you and I think we would have a great family." This was the greatest thing I had ever heard anyone say to me and she became the most influential person in my life. Her words made me believe that I could become a better person and live the life I desired. She even promised to help me with my education and help me with a career. I was so excited that I wanted to run to the courts and marry her that day.

I began looking into what I really wanted to do for a living and talking to others about the possibilities. One of the members of the church said that their auto repair shop was looking for help and I could eventually become a mechanic. This was appealing so I went and applied. Since I didn't have any experience, they started me out as a Fuel Pump Service Attendant. As time went on, I realized it would be a long time before I could make any real money before I got married so I kept looking.

I found my way into the medical field and thought that this was for sure my future as I love to help people. My wife said she didn't think that I would ever quit the nursing homes because I got so attached to the elderly. I loved listening to their stories and sound wisdom! However, I began working in hospitals and even worked some with a local fire department. One of my biggest joys was being able to be a medic and help out when a tornado hit Joplin, MO. There was so much love and care seen there that I will never forget the experience.

Finances were getting better so I finally rented a house and got out on my own. It wasn't a big place but it was enough to get started. The wedding was soon and I wanted to be ready to make a home for my new bride. I even got a job that was just a block away and could be home minutes after clocking out. April came over a few times to help me get the place decorated. The backyard was nice and big so Austin and my dog would have plenty of room to play.

The wedding day was finally here and I was nervous and excited all at the same time. The event was well organized with the help of the church. I stood at the front with my best man, Jake, and asked him what I was supposed to do next every 5 minutes. He kept me calm and said that I didn't have to worry and that everything was going to be alright. Then, there she was dressed in all white and walking up the aisle. I didn't think I would have any issues but to see her, that beautiful, caused me to get weak.

    The music was perfect and the church was packed. We read our vows and the preacher was ready to pronounce us husband and wife but I said, "Hold on!" I walked over to Austin and got down on one knee. I then read a vow to be his father and he accepted. I then walked back over to the preacher and told him I was ready. When it was all over we ran as though we were running away to our honeymoon but we snuck back in and got ready for the reception. At the reception, many great gifts to give our family a great start.

Chapter 10

Learning to Excel

"Education is the most powerful weapon which you can use to change the world" - Nelson Mandela

For the first two years of our marriage, April gave me an education. She taught me using books, workbooks, graded my papers and she even taught me how to speak well. This wasn't easy for her because I would complain that she made me feel stupid. I would apologize over and over because I would realize that it wasn't her at all. It was more like flashbacks of all my efforts in school and remembering that I was told I may have a severe learning disability. My emotions were hard to contain but she didn't quit on me and I wouldn't quit on her.

My reading had improved enough to start a book series and I started reading about kids who were living in a boxcar. I would read a little more from advanced books until I finally read a whole book. This took time but I wasn't going to give up because I truly wanted to better myself. My wife would encourage me often. She would tell me when she noticed me improving in anything. The more I read, the more my comprehension improved. After some time, I got to the point that I could understand the bible more clearly. I then started teaching bible studies.

Just when things started going great, I got a disturbing phone call. It was the gang from Las Vegas and they told me they found me and they were coming for me. I told them that I had a family and didn't want any trouble. They said they didn't care because I was never supposed to leave the gang. I thought that this was the worst thing that could happen to me but then I got another phone call. This time it was the leader of the gang from Kansas. He said he heard I left the gang and wanted to come talk with me. He told me he was going to meet me at my house.

With all of these things happening so fast, I couldn't think of what to do. I decided to go and speak with my pastor. After explaining the phone calls, I started to get mad and said, "If I see them I'm going to…" My pastor interrupted me and said, "Now, wait a minute! When you went to the altar, what did you ask God for?" I replied, "Forgiveness." Then, as he was walking away, my pastor said, "Then pray and ask God to forgive them." I was shocked. All I could think was that my pastor was not familiar with gangs and that's why he didn't give me better advice. However, I decided I would take his advice and I went home and prayed.

After a week, I got a phone call from the gang in Vegas. I was told not to worry about the gang because the leader found a church and the gang no longer exists. I hung up the phone and called to tell my pastor the news. We celebrated by giving thanks to God. Within days, the leader from the other gang showed up at my house. I went outside to meet him and I carried my bible with me. After a short bible study, he decided to start coming to church with me. The gang from Kansas broke apart and everybody went their separate ways.

Everything seemed to start getting better but I was still in need of financial stability. I was getting plenty of hours but the pay was not good enough to support my family. Even if we were struggling financially, my wife would tell me that she had confidence that I would figure it out. I told her that I wanted to be able to make enough that if she wanted to be a stay at home mom, she could. This made her happy so I immediately started looking for a way.

I got to the point where I worked three jobs and April was finally able to stay at home. We had 4 kids by this time and this allowed her to give them all of her time. This went well for a while but then I was getting worn out and we were missing each other a lot. I kept going because she and the kids were very happy but my lack of rest finally caught up to me. I was driving to my second job, fell asleep at the wheel and crashed into two cars. Everyone was okay but I realized that I was working too much and quit one of my jobs.

During this time, I was offered training to learn how to manage a restaurant with all expenses paid.

I accepted the offer and did very well on every exam. I started out being an assistant manager in a pizza shop and then went on to be the general manager of a Longhorn BBQ restaurant. I learned a lot about managing a business, managing finances and leading people. Learning the leadership skills was huge in my personal growth and has helped me in many other areas of my life. Running the restaurant was a big undertaking but I accomplished every goal, including the ability to bring the restaurant to a profitable position. The owner of the restaurant came to me and complimented me on how well I was doing but then said he needed me there all day and every day. I reminded him how important my family and church was to me and I wouldn't accept. He then told me to choose between church and the restaurant. I put in my two weeks notice and began looking for another job. The restaurant closed down shortly after I left so either way it was important for me to move on.

    I talked with my wife and said, "You know, Jim Rohn says, "Wages make you a living, which is fine, but profit makes you a fortune, which is superfine" so I think I should get into sales." She agreed that it was worth a try. I started out with network marketing and did very well. I was making so many sales that my mentor asked me to share my story with him. After I did he said, "Wow, you were relentless. Would you be willing to share that at the next event?" I agreed and began at once to prepare what I would speak.

When the next event came and it was my time to come forward, my mentor introduced me as Mr. Relentless, Jim Beach. In that moment, I realized my nickname was no longer "Retard" but now I am being called "Mr. Relentless" and I was pumped. This was good energy for my speech and the people responded well. When it was all over, people wanted to speak with me. This helped me to break out of my fear of interacting with people.

I went home and told my wife that because of all of her help with my education that I was going to give her all the things she ever desired. She told me it wasn't going to be hard because I had already covered one of her desires and that was to have a nice size family. Her only other desires were to visit NYC and drive an SUV. I promised I would make this happen and started working more on myself so that I could make these desires come true.

I started reading books on personal development and found a book on making friends and influencing people. This book helped me to realize how to improve my social skills. One of the greatest things I learned was to be more of a conversationalist, you had to be a great listener. I decided to put this into practice by going to big gatherings and events and asking questions to get people to talk. It wasn't long before I was no longer an introvert and I was able to mingle with anybody.

I was still searching for the best way to bring in enough money to give my wife those desires and came across an opportunity to take over a recycling business. This was great money and I started doing sales on the side. The money was finally coming in and I was invited to speak at many events. My wife strongly dislikes flying which made me go to many events alone. I decided that I wanted her to come along on these events. She would often have to bring the kids so I went out and bought her the first SUV that she ever wanted. I later found an opportunity to take her to NYC for an event that needed my help. We stayed for eight days and enjoyed visiting all of the historic places.

Chapter 11

Life Can Be Tough - Be Relentless

"When life knocks you down, try to land on your back. Because if you can look up, you can get up. Let your reason get you back up." - Les Brown

    I would love to say that everything has been perfect since I was beginning to realize success but that isn't reality. It seemed like life was putting us to the test and we didn't think we were going to pass. Life challenges can be so unexpected and cause you to question everything. This is when you need to remember things like faith, bible scriptures and the people who are willing to help you get through your tough times. God always knows where you are at and what you're dealing with.

    One of the biggest challenges we faced was during the time we were expecting our fifth child. We were so excited as well as our friends and family. The happiness became sadness when my wife had to let me know that she miscarried the child. I was devastated but I wasn't going to show it because I wanted to be strong for her. When others found out, the support came pouring in. April and I had talked and decided that we were going to be alright because we were blessed with four beautiful kids that are thriving. I told her that one day, we will walk into heaven's pearly gates and hear a child calling out to us saying, "Mommy! Daddy! You're here!" and it'll be the child we never met.

Not too long after that happened, we had a falling out with our church. To some, that may not be a big deal but it was for us since we had been there for over 15 years. The biggest pain was that we didn't do anything to deserve what occurred and how it was handled. Our kids were probably hurt the most as they had friends there that they knew from birth. We struggled with this but I felt that God would lead us to another church. We did not blame God so we were not going to give up on him.

During this time, I decided to get off the road to help my wife deal with all of this. I began to struggle again financially. The market was falling and my recycling business profits were driven by market values. This put a hurt on everything, especially now that the kids were older and required extra expenses. I was faced with a lot of discouragement and stress. My wife and I found ourselves arguing, more than ever, and it was all money related. It got so bad that we had to get rid of her SUV. At that moment, I decided that I was going be relentless again and go back into sales so I could control my income.

It took some time but we got back on track. I became the number one income earner from one sales company, earned the biggest bonus check from another and was asked to start speaking again. When I spoke at the event, I felt I was doing what I was meant to do. It was confirmed when I got off the stage by the many individuals that said my life story had given them hope and they were going to apply the things I taught. I thanked them and left to look for my wife.

When I found her, I noticed she was surrounded by people who were applauding her for giving me the education and encouragement to succeed. It was one of my most special moments. I was proud of her and she definitely deserved the recognition. We all need to realize how much we can influence the life of another and the impact it can have on our own.

Speaking on my experience of how personal development helps one to succeed has taken us many places. I was surprised by one of the places I was invited to speak - Las Vegas. I was once a homeless man in Las Vegas and now I am going back to inspire people for greatness. I will be able to take my family on a tour of the place where I started my journey.

What I have learned from all of my life experiences is that when one is relentless about why they live - they will be relentless about the way they live. The cost of being lazy far outweighs the price of being relentless. When life gets tough you need to have optimism and self confidence in order to keep moving forward. With the help of God, friends and a relentless determination, you can make it through life's challenges.

Lastly - There were many occasions where I wanted revenge on all those who had called me "Retard". I believed the only way to accomplish this goal was to succeed in all the areas in which they said I couldn't.

BAM! Done.

PERSONAL DEVELOPMENT SPEAKER AND COACH

Personal Development is key for anyone that wants to excel in their personal and professional life. Jim Beach is a dynamic and energetic speaker that gives his audience a new perspective on relentlessly pursuing their goals, dreams and the things in which they desire and deserve.

To book Mr. Relentless for your next event or for one-on-one coaching, contact Jim Beach at:

MrJimBeach@gmail.com

or visit his website at:

www.MrRelentless.me

Connect with Jim on these social networks:
www.Facebook.com/MrRelentless10X
www.Twitter.com/JimIsRelentless
www.Periscope.tv/MrRelentless

PROFESSIONAL REFERENCES

"Mr. Relentless is a title that encompasses the life of Jim Beach, but the influence of Jim Beach stretches far beyond the title of Mr. Relentless. Jim has an unmatched ability to touch and impact lives on an extraordinary level by sharing his personal story of triumph over adversity! He is a man of exceptional character, integrity, authenticity, and faith. Where many have failed, Jim has succeeded. Where most would have quit, Jim has persevered. I am blessed to call Jim my friend, and honored to provide my recommendation. Whether you are looking to invest in a Personal Development Coach or book a Personal Development Speaker, Jim Beach should without question be at the top of your list!"

Justin Cappon, Founder of Justin Cappon PRO

"Jim Beach is an absolutely awesome inspiration to me and so many. He has overcome so much and has a gift to inspire so many in the world; that when you are relentless in pursuing your goals and dreams, you can achieve them!"

Cynthia Bazin, President of SmartChic

"I first met Jim Beach via Periscope about 9 months ago. I recall driving to a friend's to help him out when I had Jim's Scope on and listened while I drove; Jim shared his heart wrenching and moving story of how he went from someone who was called a retard growing up, being in a gang, living on the streets, to now being known as Mr. Relentless. Without that story I wouldn't have connected to Jim. That day changed my life. Jim is an extremely courageous man whom has conquered so much to get to where he is now. Yet, knowing Jim, he's just only truly begun! I'm proud to call Jim not only a friend but a beacon of inspiration for myself as well as many others."

David Dube', Founder of OnlyOneYouNeed, Inc

"Jim Beach is one of those Guys who you cross paths with and wish you would have met him years ago. His story will Engage and Inspire you to become Relentless in the pursuit of your Dreams."

Greg "The Big Dreamer" Walker, Entrepreneur | Speaker | Author

Made in the USA
Lexington, KY
20 July 2016